Bravery & Brevity

Copyright © Edward L. Holmes II.

All rights reserved. No part of this publication may be reproduced, distributed, or transmitted in any form or by any means, including photocopying, recording, or other electronic or mechanical methods, without the prior written permission of the publisher.

ISBN-13: **978-0-578-50864-1**

Acclivity Publishing

Cover & Interior design
Edward L. Holmes II

Edward Holmes

ACCLIVITY
PUBLISHING

For those grasping for hope in endless seas of fear.

For those learning to love every hideous scar.

For the champions of unseen battles.

For the victors over anxiety

and inadequacy…

…For you…

TABLE OF THE TEMPEST

THE HOPE 1

THE HEALING 26

THE HARDSHIP 48

THE HEART 80

THE HALLEL 108

INTRODUCTION

I see you,

     Still standing after walking through one of the most difficult storms of your life. You didn't plan for it, but seemingly with a mind of its own, it made a way into your numbered days. Its winds attempted to snatch your borrowed breath and whisper lies of your demise into your ears, fill your eyes with tears and heart with fear. But … you knew better, didn't you?

     You knew all too well that pain has an expiration date and victory lives on the other side of steadfast resilience. You were wise enough to hold onto hope when the floods shook your household, and strong enough to rebuild when the waters subsided. You understood that the winds *will* relent and when they do, you'll come out stronger than you were before.

     The book you're reading? Consider it *ours*. Every page and every word. Sooner or later, we're going to go through something heavier than our feeble knees can withstand, but hold on, hope is coming. Don't you ever let go of it.

     -Edward

My parents happened to name me Edward Lee, and I look two ways before I cross one-way streets. I have two parents, two sisters, two children and too much time on my hands on Tuesday nights where inspiration writes my plights by moonlight. I love my wife like I love my text messages: saved, delivered and sent. She loves me like she loves her coffee... all day, and I take compliments like spoonfuls of cinnamon.

Every now and then, I like to think I'm a writer, a fighter for the good fight who stands up for what's right but it's needed to mention that I'm human. Honestly. Like every man made, we fail and falter yet most men master masking mistakes, making the most out of their masquerade. We've got to look right, don't we? After all, they don't have to know the dirt we grow from...

Growing up, things weren't perfect, my in-crowd was too loud, humble at home but in public, proud. The folks I loved weren't "church material" most of us broken, chokin' a lung out, tatted & tattered boys and girls looking for a way out of their misery-triggers, barreling into each other's chambers for another shot at drinking love until regret gripped the gut.

Seemingly self-centered, I was a self-sinner seeking my self's inner man and wondering where the days of "pure" were plunged. I got caught up in my various vices through the vicissitudes of life, wondering why pain perpetually pummeled my plans. A slave to addiction's demands, unable to pull from its hands and this is where my storm began...

Later in life, I knew as soon as I got through a flood or two that, like me, souls like you have survived the typhoons of bad mistakes, heartbreaks and more than a mere vessel can take. Wait. There's more for you, truly, even me. See, in the hands of our Maker we don't have to DO more, but simply be. When we realize we're soaked in the rain together we'll weather the wreckage a little bit better.

Brace for the waters, brave soul.

The rhythm of the rain arrived
to rouse the sea,
to raze the tide

THE HOPE

BRAVERY & BREVITY

The rhythm of the rain arrived to
rouse the sea, to raze the tide
while I & I within my vessel
watch the silken ocean swell
amidst the rain and thunder,
lightening split the sky asunder,
only I can stop and wonder
if my anchor's going to hold.

                                    Nasty nauseated waves
                        descend while fear precipitates
                          and reigns until the bow and I
                      are humbled by the tempest's tides
                        upon the stern, the hull to tatter
                            billow of the brine to batter
                                only I can tell the matter
                                  if this anchor holds.

Grimmest thoughts now overtake
with trembling, my hope escapes
me. Inhale despair, expel vigor,
seems as though this storm was bigger
than this feeble heart could bear,
my vessel failing, floating there
with death's door daunting, I'll declare
this anchor's going to hold.

THE HOPE

The purpose of the mainstay was
to keep my heart from failing,
yet violent winds of fear descend
upon my vessel sailing.
This ailing now prevailing
railing hard and won't withhold,
yet through the rain and cold, I know
the anchor's going to hold.

> I hold on tight with every bit
> of strength possessed upon this ship.
> No more shaken by the winds of hell
> that tell me to give in.
> A glimmer in the clouds
> has severed dark from light
> this storm will never
> last forever. Now I know
> this anchor's going to hold.
>
> *- The billow & brine*

BRAVERY & BREVITY

What if the body you hated
was the body that somebody wanted,
but instead, it's the vessel
you tussle and wrestle
and hustle to change
'cause it's just not the best.

Oh, the flabs hide the abs,
and your hair's rather drab,
a despicable mess, you confess
but the stress of maintaining
a schedule of shaving is waning
      (and why did you bother to care?)

I'll explain,
see, you need to embrace
every flaw on your face
(yes, the dimples and zits)
and the freckles that sit
right above every cheek
that raise up when you smile

THE HOPE

are beautiful. You should know
you've got to cherish that gut
(yes, the gut)
and that ugly ol' but-
ton nose, stretchy marks,
scars and bizarre mars you hide. You're

uniquely, indelibly,
wonderfully, truly
imperfectly perfect

and *that* is true beauty.

    - Frump is the new fire

BRAVERY & BREVITY

No matter what they told you
and no matter what they say,
what you say really matters
even though it sounds cliché.

Don't ever let them cover
up your lips with lies they sell.
They're all just scared of lions,
that's the truth they'll never tell.

    - Intimidation

THE HOPE

Above the concept of wishing,
and far exceeding happenstance, she stands.

She is steadfast, confident and unshakable,
proving an expected end with a tangible manifestation.

Believe in her, she holds promise of a day when those tears
cease to fall & laughter will finally burst forth from your lips once more.

- Hope

BRAVERY & BREVITY

She is wild like the flowers
in her hair, seemingly impervious
to destruction and unshakable like
the fortress she built.

The elements stop to ruminate
on her words, rain bows at her strength while
thunder claps at her innumerable victories
that command such undying attention.

She is cloaked in broken hopes and
chosen, chose sin, yet flows in gifts when needed.
She pleaded to be whole, while holding onto
that pride she possessed, which eventually needed to fall.

The Hope

Through valleys, hills, deserts, seas &
seasons, mercy sees into
the strongholds of her heart which
couldn't keep her captive much longer.

The fortress she built
that commanded such undying attention;
that pride she possessed, which eventually needed to fall
couldn't keep her captive much longer.

   - Mercy Runs

We've not been created to kindle chaos
within the confines of our minds to find
no solace in our thinking,
quickly sinking under weight and wonder,
waiting for our faith to plunder every blunder
from our memory banks.

The ability to renew the mind is a power you hold.

When we begin to master our thought patterns,
we've thereby disempowered
the toxicity of negative emotions
and inevitably, their repercussions.

- Metanoia

THE HOPE

You thought you
had to do something
to earn grace, didn't you?
Beloved, your greatest exploits could
never
be enough to earn what's already free.

See, it's not about you
and it's definitely not about me.
We couldn't shout loud enough,
apologize long enough,
cry hard enough,
preach eloquent enough,
or give enough
to be "enough".

    - You're forgiven

BRAVERY & BREVITY

Your joy was never stolen,
    it never can be.

We all have a choice to hold on,
    but that day
        I let go.

- Take hold again

THE HOPE

We think we lose whenever we
fall short of ribbons and gold
or when we trip a thousand times
is what we've always been told.

My friend, you can be well assured
to have not lost quite yet.
The only way we lose is when
we decide to quit.

- Don't you ever, ever stop fighting

BRAVERY & BREVITY

Blink.
Every time I gaze about the world
I think
the life I live is nothing more than just another
ripple in the ocean of time,
a fine line,
drops of water in a vapor,
find a way before you lose your

Life.
Temporary unfamiliarity
causes
us to stop the pace of life
and take a few
pauses to examine the stars
and breathe in.
Just remember how to cherish
all the little things within your

THE HOPE

Heart.
Soft and syncopated palpitations
inconsistent,
ceasing repetition of its motion in an instant
time is calling you out,
the end near,
time is fleeting for us all
so live your life without fear.

    - BLiNK

BRAVERY & BREVITY

Mitsakes are situations
never human lives,

like sneezing when your newborn is
finally asleep,
or turning onto one-way streets and
driving for a quarter mile past every
terrified motorist you see.

It's getting a fresh, green head
of lettuce for dinner &
wondering why your salad tastes like
cabbage three bites in.

Mistakes are failing to find your footing up the aisle
on your wedding day & forgetting what to say
after your first kiss.
Missing the shot
twice
and losing the game as the bleachers
echo your folly.

THE HOPE

It's like writing a poem and realizing
you spelled the first word wrong because
mistakes are many things,
but never
human
lives.

    - Mitsakes

BRAVERY & BREVITY

My heart grew terribly sick
from hope deferred
and leaning on
my very own
wisdumb.

Numb from
waiting, faith
abating, yet when it ends,
how beautiful are the blooms in a Tree of Life

bursting forth in its season
with the brilliance of
birth, giving
off the sweet
fragrance

of change.

- Heartsick & hopeful

THE HOPE

I can be a blessing or a curse;
a valiant chariot or your personal hearse.
I could be your sterling ally or your darkest foe.
Until you comprehend how to cherish me,
you'll never know.

> Don't get distracted!

I pen to you in urgency.
This world faces emergencies of vast and vile
murders, grief, destruction, and depravity.
Listen, we're not fighting flesh
but principalities:
hatred, death, and malice,
see, the Master has given you a specific amount of
      me.

I am your gift to use.
You are loosed to choose whether or not you share truth.
I'm always near. God forbid, aloof.

I am your key....
> Don't get distracted!

- If time could talk

BRAVERY & BREVITY

For in this moment's notice,
know this:
no discord will be yours
if you know that not everyone needs to know
everything you know,

you know?

    - Lou slips ink ships

THE HOPE

Irrespective of your skin tone,
religious observation,
political alignment,
geographical origin or
stature, there will always be
someone, somewhere who harbors contempt
for who you simply
are.

> On the other hand,
> you are an absolute
> *adventure* to a soul
> you've never met.

- Find them

BRAVERY & BREVITY

Brave.
What is the definition?
We are told, it's the heart that's bold, but
are we missing something bigger?
I sat up one night pondering the meaning
wondering, receding
deeper into definitions
of a destination not obtained.

12 A.M. met my sleepless sight
perseverating over percolated liquid life
that night. Would the bottom of the red-eye
give me insight? Is it confidence, assuredness,
a man fearless enough to pass the test?
I digress,
wrestling with unrest over the concept of
this.

Yet all I can conclude is that, even though we
are taught to believe that reckless abandon
goes hand in hand with what it means to be brave,
this is not at all what I've seen to be true.

THE HOPE

It's the young mind riddled with suicide inside
who tried life one more time today.
It's the sexual assault survivor that still
holds onto the concept of love and purity.
It's the single mother who provides
for the lives of her children in the midst of poverty.
It's the father who stays,
the sister who prays,
beloved, these are the brave.

   - *These are the brave*

BRAVERY & BREVITY

*It may not
look like much now, but.
hold onto hope.*

-

*Though it eludes
your sight today, victory is
on your horizon.*

-

*Engulfing dispair, fear
doubt, worry and anguish with
it's revealing light.*

- Bottle I

The Hope

Nasty, nauseated waves descend while fear precipitates

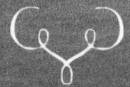

THE HEALING

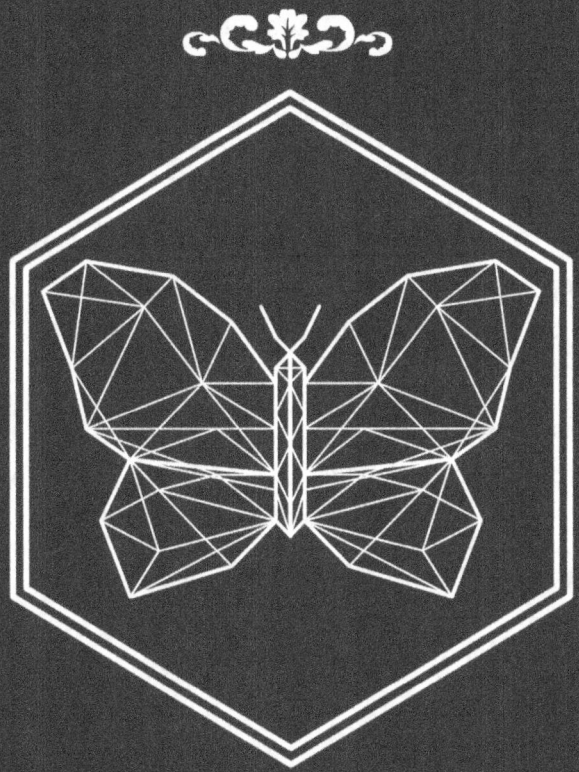

BRAVERY & BREVITY

It's easier to point a finger
at a man who's broke than pray
to God for him to have a means
to live a life above his sin.

It's easier to talk about
a man whose wife has left him for
a faithful man instead than pray
to God that he's restored someday.

It's easier to laugh and smile
at men who've fallen short of our
perception of their righteousness
than pray that God will heal their mess.

It's wiser just to keep our mouths
and commentary all about
the broken than to make another
liar out of Love, my brother.

    - We must become ambassadors
of intentional grace

THE HEALING

The moment you approached my
filthy frame
flagrant with
folly & frailty
embraced me
accepted me
and never mentioned all the cracks
was the moment that simply broke me
and finally brought me back.

- One man's trash

BRAVERY & BREVITY

There's going to come a day when you get the chance to look back
on all of this and smile.

Smile knowing that fear almost paralyzed you,
but you kept moving.

Smile knowing you lost nearly everything,
but you kept loving.

Smile knowing your health took a turn for the worst,
but you kept living.

You're going to look back on all of this and smile
because there was always greater inside of you than you had ever known.

- Cheesin'

THE HEALING

Watch for fear
and don't let him near,
    or give him the key to your home.

He'll kick off his shoes,
invite all his friends,
    and ravage your house while you're gone.

Now, when you return
you'll find it all turned
    much worse than it was right before,

so watch for fear
and don't let him near,
    or give him the keys to your door.

    - Change your locks

I wasn't sure if I was in love
with God,

or the concept of His prevenient grace
gorging itself on
my imperfections.

    - Self – ish?

The Healing

It wasn't what you did or who you were.
It was the psychological reinforcement of lies
heard from unsanctified lips, echoing
down the hallways of yesterday.

You're not a failure.
    You were never a burden.
        You are good enough,
           smart enough,
      and yes,
worthy of love.

The hardest part now
is knowing this
as truth.

- Walk in this daily

BRAVERY & BREVITY

It's a disease
and I know that it's killing you.
Been here for years
and I see that it's still in you,
stealing you,
stuck in you,
stifled, still
instilling your stagger.
The dagger
of family betrayal
they know left you unstable.
      Still trippin'

over the memories you were told
to put at ease. You're older,
a little bolder like a pebble
but colder.
Shoulders numb
from the burden of being bitter.
She was a quitter,
he was a hitter,
split your security
jaggedly down the middle.
"It'll be okay,"
they say,

THE HEALING

"Time heals all wounds."
but some decay takes decades
 or more to restore.

Healing is coming,
running to overtake the bitter
and our strength will rise,
so let her lead you down that corridor
once more for grace and mercy unlock the door
and forgiveness soothe that heart of yours, it's true.

Behold.
    Be held.
        Be healed &
            press through.

   - Topical time treatment

BRAVERY & BREVITY

There was never such a thing as
"too far gone."

Start over and don't worry
about what they think.

THE HEALING

It's not your fault,
but for so long you've heard it from
everyone else that you started to believe it.
People make choices
and hurting *you*
was theirs.

You've been trying to
wash away stains that you were never
strong enough to clean.
You were created to be spotless
and that job
       is His.

    - Blameless

On top of every hill, and
below every green canopy
sat I in temporary comfort of
my idola
trees

until my season changed,
and my shade began to
fade in the presence of this newfound light.

- *Luminous*

The Healing

Remember when they cast blame
to create shame?
You've been changed
so the old name
doesn't fit the frame.
They'll deny things
that you overcame,
not the same, so
remember that your past name
is not your last

name.

- White stones & new names

She's
got the kind
of spirit that makes
midnights
mirror
mornings.
Baby, don't you
ever let 'em
dim your
shine

- Glow, girl, glow

THE HEALING

You're not shaken,
  forsaken or left to die,
    overtaken by life's turbulent tide,
      choking through the blow of the undertow.

          Know that coming back to shore at times
           takes emergeny measures to rescue you
            from personal pride and pleasures.
             Hold your breath, son
              God's not done.

- Over my head.

Flesh to thorn and thorn to flesh
blood to bear my selfishness.
Tender soles and souls to tend
healing bought and pain to end.

    - Crux

THE HEALING

Have enough self-esteem to say
"no"
to the things gratify, yet abandon nourishment
"yes"
to what waters your soul for a better tomorrow &
"goodbye"
to anyone or anything that causes your
hope to wilt.

- The words that shape your life

BRAVERY & BREVITY

It's commonplace to sour the face,
then pout and talk about
the problematic lives we live than
wear a smile.

So wear a bright visage
that shines and shows appreciation
for the life we get to live amidst
our trials.

It's true this world has many woes
and pain will never falter
while it's showing us how easily
we b r e a k.

So, grin and grimace greatly
even when your hope's escaping
and you'll see that trials,
a stronger man,
will make.

- Roads less traveled

THE HEALING

The fact that she trusts you
plunges deeper than her words allow.
She is exposing a portion of her soul.

You weren't there when trust was
stolen, but you may be the last to
repair it.

    - Lost & found

*Your silken wings
are a product of isolation,
consecration and maturation.*

-

*In order to
heal and grow, separation was
an unavoidable choice.*

-

*They won't recognize
you, beloved. Perhaps, that's what
had to happen.*

- Bottle II

The Healing

Grimmest thoughts now overtake
with trembling, my hope escapes me

THE HARDSHIP

BRAVERY & BREVITY

Unforgiveness, how can I address this
taste on my pallet? Bitterness, I'll confess it.
Memories want to envelope my mind, ever recent,
they return, are re-sent, the reason is resent.

You were there, young heart when I met her.
I loved her, but let her be bitter than become better.
Perusing over poetic pages of read letters but
instead I should have led her to live in the red letters.

You were there when the mail I was needing
walked out, first class, since he didn't feel like leading
me the right way,
so I took trust and boxed it.
Hid it away, tucked in a corner as if I
"lost it."

But people are people and pain's in the past.
I'm stamping the letter that kills for the
Spirit to pass
and give new life, I'm
signed, sealed, delivered again.
With arms wide open I'm letting true
forgievness rush in.

THE HARDSHIP

Unforgiveness, I can now address this
box full of bitter broken things, I detest it!
Return to sender, please take this pride
for how can I truly be delivered
with the past inside?

- Bitter little boxes

BRAVERY & BREVITY

Twelve.

There were twelve tallies total that
told a story she'd be writing for years by now.

Fighting through tears, fears falling from dim eyes,
she cries for someone to read every line,
so she writes the nights away.

She writes
      and writes
and writes
      frustrations deeper than you've felt before.

Chapter 1: The abuse began.
Chapter 2: It's probably normal.
Chapter 3: What if she tells?
Chapter 4: Will they believe her?
Chapter 5: They ~~believe her~~ *don't*.
Chapter 6: PTSD is born.
Chapter 7: Forlorn from family.
Chapter 8: Too taboo for churches too.
Chapter 9: Rejection.
Chapter 10: Persistence.
Chapter 11: Resilience.
Chapter 12: She's finally found a way to ~~cut~~ cope.

THE HARDSHIP

Twelve.

His fingers felt twelve tallies
she'd been writing for years when He held her close.

Dashes dotting each arm;
morose code sending a signal of s.o.s. her mess
-age received.

He heals
      He heals
He heals
      scars deeper than she's ever felt before.

    - Raise her

It's harder than you imagined,
I know.

You woke up with its weight
wooing you deeper into gravity's grip.
Such heaviness you've hidden so well
for so long
from so many
because this year, everyone's counting on you to be
strong, aren't they?

It's going to be hard.
It's going to bend you,
But when you come out as gold,
baby, it's gonna be worth it.

    - So refined

THE HARDSHIP

A gossip loves a rumor
but a rumor never tells
what the truth is in the matter
but he "knows" the matter well.

With fabricated details fixed on
forged and faulty facts,
once the words have left a gossip's lips
he cannot take them back.

So keep your tongue from evil
and your lips from telling lies.
Without the wood a fire starves
and that's how gossip dies.

  - Juicy

BRAVERY & BREVITY

You were sitting by her every Sunday
but you never noticed
she was going through some problems,
you were too busy to focus
on what mattered. Looking at her now
I wish I would've taken
my chances to love her honestly
& demonstrate.

Instead we get it twisted
and miss it amidst the service,
too preoccupied with worshipping worship
to even notice
pain that's propped up in our pew
that we're losing sight of the mission.
Got me wishing I'd have
      saved
            her
                  life
from the mortician.
    - Can I (please) get a witness?

The Hardship

I'm unsure if I'm unsure,
not sure If I'm on shore.
My soul will tread the desert
for the oceans I adore.

My claustrophobic dreams now drown
the screams of limitation,
with soothing siren songs
that shatter ships of hesitation.

- Boundless

BRAVERY & BREVITY

A toxic soul-tie
is still
a toxic soul-tie

no matter how much they
speak of good religion.

Bonds
are still
bonds

even if the ropes
are golden.

    - Let them go

THE HARDSHIP

The cold floor swallowed my tears
as though expecting such foolish lament.
Late nights turned into mournings
with lukewarm coffee and a side of
shame carved into my mind
by two of the filthiest hands.

And I will tell myself the age-old lie
"I… can't do this again."
And I will spit-up the same prayer
"Just forgive me, again." Then
with a devil's duping delight, day becomes night
and the cold floor swallows my tears
as though expecting such foolish lament.

I have to ask myself…
"Are you tired yet?"

> *- Vice*

the pen slams the page
the black dots don't belong
never have never will
but you ink the notes still
and compose your ***own*** song
though you know this is wrong
but you still write along
when the song is complete
all the ink starts to bleed
realize you don't need
what you thought and perceived
but it aches dull and long
nauseating and strong
to compose such a thing
that you can't even sing
every note is off key
there's no rest none to see
only God knows the way
to compose a new day,
so you pray…

- Decompose

THE HARDSHIP

The deepest sinkhole has eluded the eyes
of common man, yet,
after many expeditions of the soul,
it was discovered in the center of the jilted
        s o n.

- Voids

BRAVERY & BREVITY

The shadows that I face tonight,
I cannot seem to pierce.
With lies and hate, they capsulate.
How numerous! How numerous!

I cannot seem to pierce
the sins that break Your heart.
How numerous! How numerous!
Oh, chamber dank and dark.

The sins that break Your heart
come quickly to my soul.
Oh, chamber dank and dark,
the light of prayer will pierce.

Come quickly to my soul
my Lord, do not delay.
the light of prayer will pierce
the shadows that I face tonight

- Pantoum of petition

THE HARDSHIP

The endless effort to obtain outer righteousness,
has silenced many voices of the afflicted.

Yet another drug relapse, but he needs grace.
    She loves a woman, but no one asked about the abuse.
The addiction is eating his body away.
    She never loved her body anyway.
He doesn't believe you'll accept him.
    Her family's already rejected them.

They don't need personal justification to the
shallow, but relatively accurate presupposition of cold
religion.

Brother,
start with love;
crazy,
uncomfortable,
awkward,
unconditional,
boundary-breaking,
breath-taking,
love.
    - Demonstrate

BRAVERY & BREVITY

And when you go through hell, come
back with a fist full of
embers
clutched close to your
members. Embody the
cinders and harness the sparks
'cuz
they're gonna need a navgator soon
in a world so dark.
Light the way,
burning one.

- *Torches*

THE HARDSHIP

No one knows about this emptiness,
yet your soul is starving for the type of embrace
she will never be able to provide.

Soon, the rush will be
       gone.

She'll be there tomorrow, though,
ready to make a fool out of a good man
once more.

    - Click

BRAVERY & BREVITY

"I don't need anyone else," I said to myself.
It was already a quarter past midnight, streets
shimmering to the cadence of the rain.
Pain still filled my selfish will while guilt pushed two feet
as far as they could carry me.
from You.

"I'm fine on my own," I said, alone,
walking past illuminated homes. Knowing I had only
been shown unending kindness,
my mess made of mindless ambitions clouded my sight
that night keeping my heart
from You.

"I've no regrets," I said, cold and wet,
down streetlight-lined sidewalks towards the gate. This
late,
no one would wait
for me to be safe, so why stay anyway?
My shame and I; the renegade and runaway
from You.

THE HARDSHIP

"I can't see home from here..."
        stopping,
                sobbing,
                        trembling,
nothing near to me resembling anything reminiscent
of home, yet hearing one familiar tone
of voice behind my back,
to remind me of this very simple fact:
"Son, you can't flee far enough from My arms."

- And I dropped my shame along the way back

He began to view himself
with enough self-respect
that her touch was no longer
a viable venue of validation
for his broken masculinity.

- And he walked in liberty

THE HARDSHIP

Since her first breath
she has always been more than men's perception
of perfection somewhere between likes and
comment sections,
    but she never feels that way.

And with every filter, she's spilled her
life out for the masses' approval
to remove all doubt that she's even beautiful,
    but she's skeptical. Still

trafficking life's joy for the mouths of boys
voracious for a couple ribs to satisfy sight's appetite.
If she performs a little harder they'll love her,
    right?

She's developed
the ideal frame with
a hunger for exposure just to keep all the negatives at bay,
made in the very image of her Creator
    but she never felt that way.

    - *More likes, tho*

BRAVERY & BREVITY

H.D. flat screen.
Perfect Pixel LCD.
Tick, tap, clicky-clack,
forging fantasy, a snap.
Cold stare, in a chair,
hours passing unaware.
Brain-dead, nothing said,
pupils slowly turning red.
Make, mesh, melt and mold,
in this world he has control.
Nothing bends and nothing breaks
except the time that he forsakes.
Hack, crack
This and that.
More to see and
Less to be,
searching hard
& never free
to be the man
he's made to be.

- The lie of technology

THE HARDSHIP

Sometimes
I wonder how the snake acquired
such a diabolical reputation, don't you?

She's wise enough to know that
she never has to return to what has been outgrown:
the dead shells of "once was"

and "used to be"
have fallen off
and set her free.

    - Shrewd

BRAVERY & BREVITY

Setting out
to sail the seas
and venture the unknown,

yet all she found
were daunting waves
that forced her voyage home.

Stepping out
to climb the peaks
that none had scaled before,

yet all she found
were frigid gales
that froze ambition's core.

Running wild
to ancient lands
for riches none have owned,

yet all she found
was failure searching
hungry and alone.

THE HARDSHIP

Launching forth
to find a love
that cures an empty soul,

yet all she found
were broken men
that never made her whole.

Writing in
her rocking chair
the past has proved for sure,

that every blessing
might be held
if only she endured...

   - *Miss adventure*

BRAVERY & BREVITY

Why make it seem so impossible
for the King of all
to add peace to this puzzle and

why do my ramblings run on and on?
Verbal toil and song
as we're singing it, ringing it

louder than He's ever asked us to be.
The King tries to whisper as we shout "defeat!"
A palm ever pure reaches out just to find
such a multitude eager to leave Him behind.

Flags waving high, negative of noir
seen from near and far
waving captive surrender.

Impatient sensations are raging strong.
"I can't wait that long!"
It's so easy to quit when

He's folding us, molding us, making us mighty.
Instead burning passions have tempted the flighty.
The grave pants and beckons, we court worms and bones
while we wonder why we've always felt so alone.

THE HARDSHIP

Why do we act so ridiculous?
Ever scandalous,
as if Yahweh can't handle this?

Why do we veil what is obvious
while He's near to us?
We inhale our lusts till we bust.

I've tried to bend, break, mask-over and hide.
A symptom to suffer when living in pride.
Omniscient He's standing there right by our side
waiting for us to come clean in the light.

Waiting for you.

Waiting for me.

Open our eyes Lord to finally see.

- I'm patient

BRAVERY & BREVITY

A dollar can be stolen,
a house, a car;
they'll break in.

    Thieves plunder possessions,

and for a time we wonder
if we'll ever reclaim
what we've lost,

    but wouldn't it be beautiful

if we all invest in
the treasures that no evil
can rend from our hands?

    To diligently protect

love, a dream,
our hope and our will.
Perhaps, could this be

    true wealth?

    - What cannot be stolen

The Hardship

All hell rose, but so did he
to stand against adversity
with unrelenting hope to see tomorrow,
torment had to flee
from where it took its residence
within the mind. The evidence
of confidence was growing, hence
the exit of its decadence.

- Free thought

*There were days
when the weight of "why"
would wake you,*

-

*shake you from
your rest, purloining peace from
your tender heart.*

-

*Remember that today
is not eternity. Every heartbreak
has to end.*

- Bottle III

The Hardship

THE PURPOSE OF THE MAINSTAY WAS TO KEEP MY HEART FROM FAILING

THE HEART

The ability to love people is a violent opposition to a
world that propogates vengeance.

With every lifted stone, I'll choose to
allow silent defiance to eradicate the walls between us.

Be still, and let a forgiving heart drive your
every enemy to shame.

    - Solus amor

THE HEART

Her path is never crooked,
she is straight and true.

The arrow that never misses her mark,
perpetually
peircing and
pushing her
pin-
point
promises
deeper and deeper
into desperately wicked hearts
until every bit of hatred is convicted to bleed
from sanctuaries never constrcuted for it.

Her path is never crooked,
she is straight and true.

    - And she is love.

BRAVERY & BREVITY

We all want love, but
many times we're unsure of how
to pluck its sweetness from the branches
we're all too afraid to climb. The bark will greet
your palms with splinters. The branches may be a
little brittle, it'll certainly break under the weight of
your baggage, and ~~if you fall~~ when you fall, you'll
have to start over. You'll lose your footing,
heart-in-throat, holding on with all of your
might at times, but friend if you must
know, it will be worth
the climb.
You
can
taste
every
apple
you
desire
without
the
axe.

- Branching out

THE HEART

You're going to experience a day
when the words "I love you" will hold
      so
      much
      weight
leaving your lips,
spilling over your teeth and
freezing you by the
freedom they've found in a soul so
very
faithful.

That day will come,
and it's just the beginning
of many more.

    - Love unending

We want to be loved, don't we?
Yet, sometimes (okay, more often than not)
we don't do things that are conducive to receiving it.

How can I ask for that which
  I refuse to embody?
How can I expect
  what I don't give?

Perhaps I should represent
what I need first.

> *- Love is an echo*

THE HEART

Learning to
love who
you are
in the
middle of
every ugly
secret you've
tried to hide
is how
you'll learn to
love them.

    - Mirrors

BRAVERY & BREVITY

She was Helvetica
in a room full of Comic Sans.
That's how I knew she was
my type.

I could see the Futura from
an Arial view.
Times were changing ~~for me
and you.~~ You and I, too.
I had to check the spell
that you had us under,
lines locked forever never sever asunder.

The Impact of your passion lost me in a forest of
poetries. She was a metaphor,
and now I know what
I met her for.

- I think this will rock well

THE HEART

Love shouldn't hurt.

It should ache,
groan deep within us
long and strong without
relenting. It must
fight for walls to fall
around you, resounding
through from start to finish
and replenish hope where
doubt tried to discount you both.
Let it cover your shame with
grace and mercy
bursting with forgiveness
firstly.

Let it ache.
Let it last longer
than you ever wanted it to.

> *- But, oh, it must be felt*

Your singularity
will never be synonymous with
incompleteness.

    You are enough.

Forcing that poor heart of yours to
endure a relationship of any sort
in order to feel "whole," of course
is a dangerous thing to resort to.

    You are enough.

It's time to be gentle to the heart crafted within your chest.

Go out for coffee &
    be sure to give frequent compliments.
(You know you deserve them)

Don't wait to take that vacation, leave next month &
make memories that will last for years to come.

THE HEART

Go to the movies and laugh until you cry,
and if they ask you to be quiet, laugh harder.

(You'll be escorted to the parking lot, but you can laugh about that later, too)

Then watch the parts you missed on Blu-ray
    with vanilla ice cream
        and footie-pajamas
            because no one can judge you.

- One is happy too

We tend to run to
what gives us life,

    chase what fills
    our lungs with air,

        pursue whom makes
        us feel secure.

            Be sure you're the life,
            air, and security to your lover.

- *Life. Air. Security.*

THE HEART

She is worth fighting for
even if you don't always get
what you want.
      (You won't)
My friend, love was never about
getting.

Now, here's the part where you would assume
that I'll say love is all about giving,
but you'd be wrong, still.

It's about relentlessly proving over
and over
and over
that there's still a man capable
of navigating the fog of war for
her battle-scarred heart.

    - Pursuit

BRAVERY & BREVITY

You have options.
You've got backup plans, security nets
and trump cards just in case your
current situation doesn't pan out
the way you'd like it to. You've got them,
and so do I.

We have options
which, frankly, just might be the root
of our deep, deep dissatisfaction &
destructive decisions.

- The perpetual problem of the plethora

THE HEART

Good hearts still exist in this world.
They do.

Gentle hearts.
Faithful hearts.
Forgiving hearts.
Empathetic hearts.

If we change the way we observe the world around us,
we may find that good hearts are often
closer than we think.

- And this requires a bit of altruism

Love is not a partial thing
it has to be the whole or
else the love you choose to
give could leave a bigger hole.

THE HEART

Love and shame cannot exist
within the same room,
one has to
die.

The
shame you hold
will kill your love, but love
has the power to execute all shame.

- And here we are, in the fray

Love arrived with baby's breath
and rose to conquer sin and death.
Sunday morning glory taught
my heart You are
forget-me-not.

    - The garden

THE HEART

He once told me to
keep them close.

Like a father embraces his first newborn
as though he's capable of making the moment
halt
and try to bask in its walls forever.

To keep them like the Almighty has a hold
on the hearts of His children,
like every prayer their lips have ever uttered
to heaven in precious bowls like incense
since the precious day of adoption.

He once told me to keep them close
                     and today I believe every word.

    - Family

Be careful never to lace your heartstrings
to a soul
that disrespects you with their tongue.

Such a person will trample your emotions
as if nothing's afoot.

   - Heels found are in more places than bread

THE HEART

You didn't lose him,
it was always in his gaze
to walk away
to go astray
to catch your eye and drop a lie.

You never had him,
it was always in his feet
to make retreat
to live deceit
to play the game and try to cheat.

- Half-hearted

When you're ready,
step into the
d
  e
l
  u
g
  e
of authentic love. It will drown
the damaging accusations
of all lingering insecurities,
silencing the genesis of each syllable
with the power of inaudible

‖ pauses ‖

that cause this heart to know
agapeo's undertow.

    - *I choose not to swim*

THE HEART

We're living in a day where many an
   "I love you" cannot be received
prior to investigation.

Often
the recipient has received
far too many fraudulent phrases from
phonies to be confident with just another

"I love you."

    - Returned to sender

BRAVERY & BREVITY

Mama tried to cook each night
and never missed a meal.
We ate from plates she washed that day
until our guts were filled.

Mama tried to pay each bill
so we could have a place
where lights were running all year round,
where we could wash our face.

Mama tried to discipline
and never spare the rod
so we could grow to break the mold,
statistics, we were not.

Mama tried to educate
our young minds to be strong
enough to have discernment and
to know our right from wrong.

Mama tried protecting us
from choices that would steal
our innocence and confidence
that love was truly real.

THE HEART

The most important thing I learned
now seeing through her eyes:
I'd grow to be a better man
because I learned to try.

    - Mama tried

*Out of all the
miracles God could perform with
the hearts of men,*

-

*the most powerful
will be His revealed love
for His children.*

-

*It echoes from
heart to heart, as the
evidence of God.*

- Bottle IV

THE HALLEL

BRAVERY & BREVITY

In my mind's a truth that casts
away my deepest fear:
praying to the Father knowing El Shaddai is near.
To understand the Great I Am
has planned this from the start
and knows the pangs and yearnings
that reside within my heart.
(Jeremiah 29:11)

In my own remembrance,
a physician, set apart:
My Creator bound my wounds,
and healed my broken heart.
You told me I'm protected
when the pain was much to bear,
reminding me You're GOD and that
You always truly care.
(Psalm 147: 3)

The Hallel

In my own confusion
lies a Truth beyond compare:
despite the ways the world portrays,
I know You're always there.
When wrapped within the darkness
in the dead of night I am,
I can't be overtaken,
with my life now in your hands.
(John 14:6)

And in my foolishness,
so brash and young I seek You still.
Your steps, my feet shall follow,
light my path to see Your will.
And though I'm weak and lowly,
to a King my life is vowed.
I pray, my Father, use me
to confound the wise and proud.
(1Corinthians 1:27)

- To my remembrance

How easily we trip into the trap of believing that
there is something we must perform to become
more significant in the eyes of our Creator.
We tell ourselves we've made our election sure,
while holding onto the erroneous belief that we're only
worth pursuing when we're "good."

But we are not God.
We have never been able to harness the power of
salvation in our tiny hands, nor are we able to determine
the worth of another.

It's here that I fully understand that we are loved
not because we've done something "good," but because
of whom we belong to.

- And this is the ridiculous truth of adoption.

THE HALLEL

I can't live without You & I forever

nor can I live without You & die forever.

   - One way out

BRAVERY & BREVITY

The King confounded the multitudes
with His cross words.
They weren't dross words,
eloquent or false words.
He said "forgive them,"
but we live as if we've not heard.
Like it's a game, boyish ways have made us absurd.

The sour wine was given,
now our wine is living
inside. My provision
is Thine. I'm forgiven!
I'm so blessed to be covered and stained.
He bled from His hands, never once in vain.

For all the hate that we've hidden
He was our hang-man,
erasing pain that can lock us up in shame
and
brought us to blessed perfection
to heal our vain land.
Christ made it plain, now He reigns at the right hand.

THE HALLEL

The Bread of Life was broken,
so now my heart is spoken
for. Heaven's earth-collision
declaring I'm forgiven!
I'm so blessed that to be covered and stained.
He bled from His hands, never once in vain.

The King of Hearts departed
to open paradise,
so why consider to gamble
it like pair of dice?
The hand was dealt, fear was felt,
when the veil was sliced.
Sweet breath ascended and mended
a path from broken life.

- Crossword Christianity

BRAVERY & BREVITY

Our conversations as of late have been
poignant reminders of unending grace,

and I, doing everything in my power,
trying to convince You I don't deserve it.

    - But I simply can't

THE HALLEL

You enthrall me
in a manner unexplainable.
When you call me,
how I stammer to sustain it all.
Ever stoked
With flames of fire deep inside of me.
Infinitely,
intimately, I have been redeemed.

    - The purchase

It's in the moments when pain has pressed its
fingers
deeper
than I'd ever imagined into
my life, that I realize my deep inner need
for salvation.

For me, it was never a rescue from this world
or its faculties,
but myself.

> - *The villain of my heart*

THE HALLEL

I catch glimpses of You
in strangers that leave me

                              longing.

Such simple split-second-sights
leave me *frantic* when You

                              abandon

me for the next vessel as I grasp
for stability with raw fingertips to a crumbling world.

I can stand.
If for only a time,
I could only see Your face clearly and know,
would I be satisfied?
How could I be?
The moment would be far too much to withstand.
So instead, I'll wait…
to catch more glimpses.

- As we give chase

BRAVERY & BREVITY

On my face was where I needed to be,
eating the very substance of which I am made of
before You, to adore You and assure You that
 I. Am. Full. Of. Sin-
cerity.

It was clear that I needed to
when I noticed You,
ever pure and true,
yet my mask hid me from the furnace
that burns us and refines me to be who I am.

The call for acceptance as a teenager would
reach my pager and make wagers for my personality.
See, commonality was conformity marketed by
non-conformists, pressing their beliefs on a broken boy
with no identity.
So I picked up my mask, knowing my task wouldn't last
and I started to blend.

THE HALLEL

There I was,
locking arms with screamers, blasphemers,
liars, thieves, and adulterers.
But it's cool…
They *love me,* which is why they
abused me
and used me to buy their cigarettes, liquid regrets, and contracep-
tives.

Yet I thought I was supposed to be
a man of pure integrity
with everything inside of me
I fell so hard I couldn't see through my
cussin' profanity,
vanity-bred insanity.
Purity: my anomaly.
Sin was secreting over me.
Playing risk with the enemy.
Bitterness was a friend to me.
Anger was all that I could see
through this mask

BRAVERY & BREVITY

On my face
was where I needed to be,
eating the very substance of which I am made of.
Your face defined me, yet I feared You.

Love was a four-letter word spelled backward when I met her.
She was clever and fair,
long flowing hair,
smells like Marlboro,
tastes like regret.
So, I picked up my mask, knowing my task wouldn't last
and I started to blend

There I was...
locking eyes with a swift woman
that would make the Painted Whore of Babylon blush.
Two feet in the grave,
I lingered on every word said
in my head, not knowing she would eventually
love me dead,
reducing me to a crust of bread.
But it's cool…
She loves me,
which is why she inquired of me to forfeit my purity
and when she tried,

The Hallel

I denied,
so she lied,
throwing me to the side.
Real love was on my agenda
but this girl was just a pretender.
I needed a real defender
but instead I became a spender of my flesh.
Bankrupt of joy, with my savings full of suicidal thoughts
and plots
that I bought
from her market of lusts.

On my face
was where I needed to be,
eating the very substance of which I am made of.
Your face defined me, yet I feared You.

Abandoned as a boy,
frankly, father failed to fit the foreground,
like five "F's" on my report card,
loving self was especially hard,
so I hated every pore of the man whom my own flesh reflected.
Run child, from a severed roof to a place I could call my own... to be someone unlike he,
and like a prodigal fool, I had begun to

BRAVERY & BREVITY

idolize with
idol eyes the
idle lies
of mother mammon.
The world was beautiful
but I was not. I was taboo so
like glue I attached my mask,
knowing my task wouldn't last
and I started to blend.

Money's embrace, I would chase,
adorning my body with piercings
and things that gave me a false sense
of confidence, riding the fence,
I was dense.
Nappy roots weren't "cute"
my intellect: moot,
feeling ugly to boot
so I fought to change the unchangeable
with pocket change.

Filling my flesh with more rocks was what I needed,
so I sought diamonds and gold
and whatever I was told was fresh and fly
for a coy black boy.
But it's cool…

THE HALLEL

money *loves* me.
Which is why her presence was rare.
She left my wallet bare,
changed my hair
and a heart that used to never care
about appearance.
Yet, through this mask, all I could see was my own greed
making me bleed
and stain my clothes with the
unsatisfactory view of unaccepted and
rejected skin & flesh.

On my face
was where I needed to be,
eating the very substance of which I am made of.
Your face defined me, yet I feared You.

Then one day on my daily jog through
hell on earth, I tripped over self and ran into You.
I could not avoid You,
escape You,
ignore You,
define You,
comprehend You,
all I *could* do is fall on my face where I needed to be.
You told me that I was made in the image of You,

beautifully and wonderfully true,
that my fingerprints echo the hands of God
and my heart keeps the rhythm to
the song of adoption.

Ab-ba…
                Ab-ba…
    Ab-ba…

YOU are my Heavenly Father,
so why would I bother a world of
dead-
        beat
                daddies in the form of luxuries?

You took off my masks,
allowing me to see the very man of which I am made from.
My face set like flint,
I've been defined and I fear You
Oh! How I fear You and
desire to be near You!
Your love is what I run to,
so I say "thank You!"

THE HALLEL

You are who I need.
You are who I seek.
Who I love.
Who I live for,
who is so much more

than a mask.

  - Masks

BRAVERY & BREVITY

Take my sight
    & watch my faith grow.
Take my vision
    & buy a headstone.

The Hallel

I am the water at Cana
I am the pool of Bethesda
I am the river of Jordan
I am the lake of Gennesaret
I am the sea of Galilee

You are Mirth
You are Healing
You are New Life
You are Abundance
You are the Voice of Peace

> *- Let my life saturate*

BRAVERY & BREVITY

I'm not afraid of the tempest & flow.
No longer timid and limited, no!

Grabbing the rein,
breaking the chain,
breathing again,
call it insane.

You had a grip like a ship on the rocks.
Won't understand but I stand under God.

I found the key,
fearless and free,
now I can see
who I'm destined to be.

I'll never sway to you,
look what I'm made to do:
pounding the pen for the
broken still bleeding through.

THE HALLEL

People that ponder their
life when the rent is due.
Those under steeples still
searching for what is True.

Brothers that feel so
rejected and pitiful.
Sisters who can't rise
above all the ridicule.

Body of death, I
declare you dismissible,
vincible, fallible,
now I know what is true.

Death has been wrecked by a
King and His message, the
torment of cancer will
answer to Yeshua.

Racism, hatred, and shame
have been swallowed up
followed up quickly by
glory. We're rising up

higher above every
chain that had bound us
around us, He found us,
adopted and crowned us.

So I'm not afraid if
the Master can save.
Teach me to tread on the
crest of the wave.

> *- War cries & open skies*

THE HALLEL

Unlock the window pane.
Love's rushing in like a hurricane,
ruin the walls in our hearts.
Rearrange every strange and
peculiar thing that can cause
us to sever or keep us apart
and allow every gale, every gust as it gathers
to shift move and bust every beam as it batters these
bricks made of bitter and hallways of malice
to radically alter our self-righteous palaces.

    - Gale

*Sudden storms will
come to shake your soul.
Don't let go.*

-

*Pain will rain
down suddenly with no remorse.
Don't let go.*

-

*Though water fills
your vessel, don't let go,
salvation is coming.*

- Bottle V

The Hallel

Dear reader,

My Name is Edward Lee Holmes, the author of Bravery & Brevity and other works. If I could shake your hand, or rather, hug your neck, I would.

Life is hard. Period.
We're going to go through circumstances that have the capacity to strengthen us or tear us apart, so I hope the art form and vehicle of poetry has in some way encouraged you today.

This book was birthed out of many of those life experiences, both sweet and sour. I too have felt the hand of addiction, anxiety attacks, fear, cold religion, shame, discrimination and betrayal. It's going to rain upon the sinner and saint, so grab your umbrella.

I pray that whatever is breaking your heart in this season is beneath you in the next. It'll change. It won't always be this way, trust me.

Cling to healthy counsel.
Care well for your heart.
Pray without ceasing.

   - Your friend and biggest fan,
    Edward

Edward Holmes is an American author and speaker with an evangelist's heart and a poetic pen.
It's his life mission to encourage others that the darkest corners are life are *still* worth living through his writing, ministry and speaking engagements.

You can connect with him and more of his work on:

Instagram: @Edwardlee_on_ig
Facebook: @Edwardlee423
Twitter: @EdwardLHolmes

EdwardLHolmes.com

Acknowledgements

Almighty *God*, for sufficient grace and strength to have carried me through many of the situations expressed in this very book.

My incredible wife, for believing in me, especially when I don't believe in myself.

Dr. Kitty Bickford
for your patient guidance and wisdom.

Coffee (The Real MVP)

And *You. Yes, YOU,* my friend. Thank you for considering this work something of value.

It may seem like we're going to sink, but I can assure you...

The Anchor Holds

THE END

"He calmed the storm to a whisper and stilled the waves."

Psalm 107:29

www.ingramcontent.com/pod-product-compliance
Lightning Source LLC
Chambersburg PA
CBHW051402290426
44108CB00015B/2125